The Eg

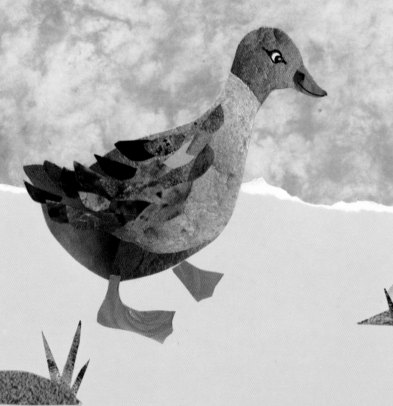

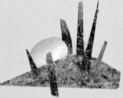

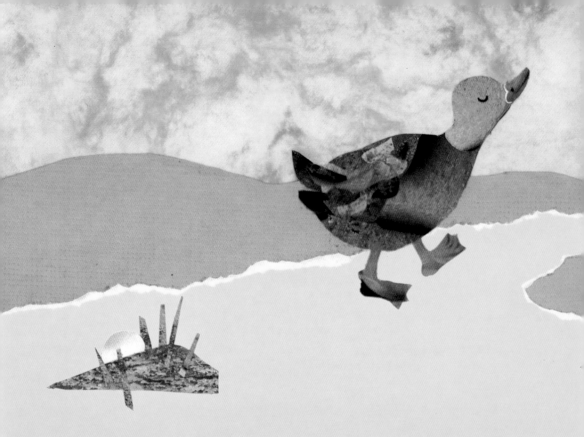

"It is not my egg,"
said the duck.

2

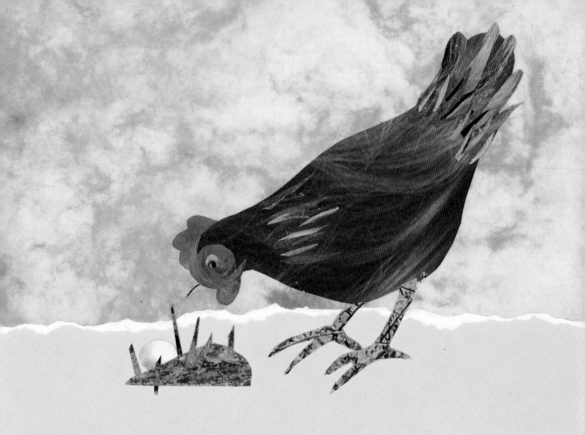

"It is not my egg,"
said the hen.

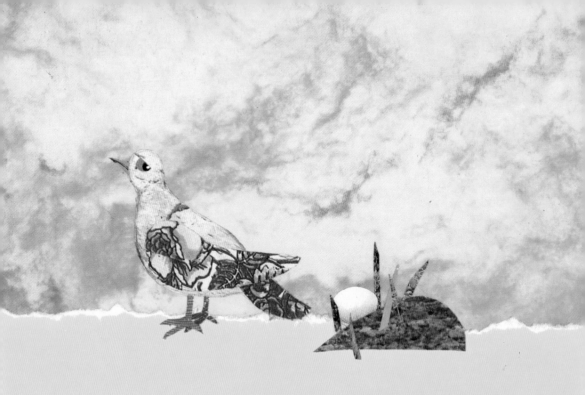

"It is not my egg,"
said the pigeon.

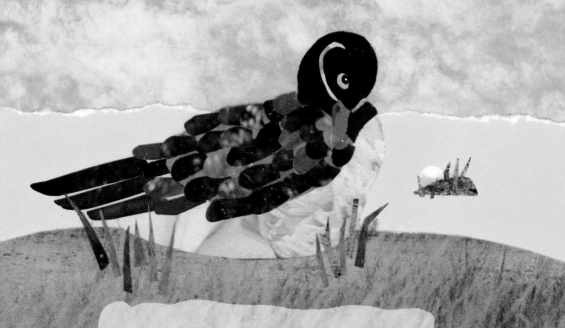

"It is not my egg,"
said the goose.

5

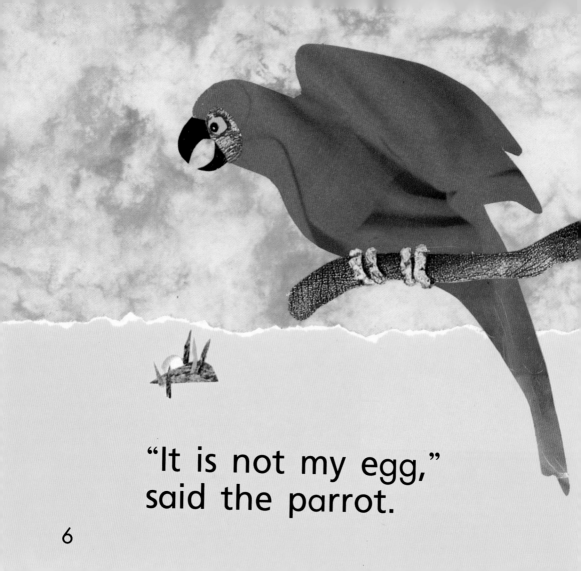

"It is not my egg,"
said the parrot.

6

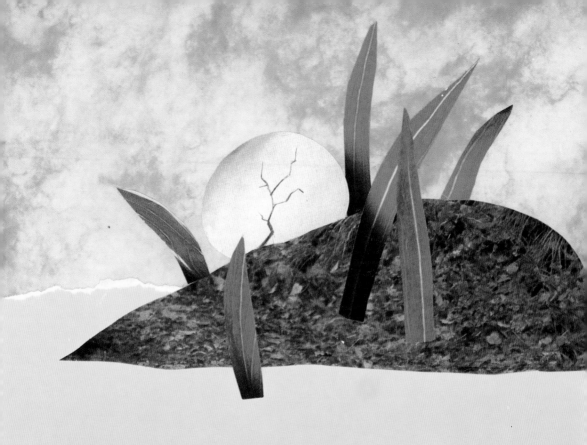

Crack!

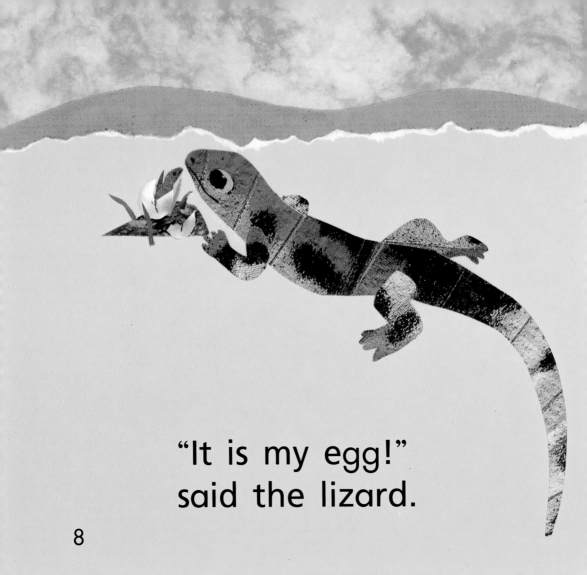

"It is my egg!"
said the lizard.